MW00795322

GRATITUDE

POEMS OF
LIFE AND LOVE

Kathryn Carole Ellison

KATHRYN CAROLE ELLISON

Published by Lady Bug Books, an imprint of Brisance Books Group.
Lady Bug Press and the distinctive ladybug logo are registered trademarks of
Lady Bug Books, LLC.

Lady Bug Books
400 112th Avenue N.E.
Suite 230
Bellevue, WA 98004
www.giftsoflove.com

For information about custom editions, special sales and permissions, please contact
Brisance Books Group at specialsales@brisancebooksgroup.com

Manufactured in the United States of America
ISBN: 978-1-944194-60-4

First Edition: November 2019

A NOTE FROM THE AUTHOR

The poems in this book were written over many years as gifts to my children. I began writing them in the 1970s, when they were reaching the age of reason. And, as I found myself in the position of becoming a single parent, I wanted to do something special to share with them—something that would become a tradition, a ritual they could count on.

And so the Advent Poems began—one day, decades ago—with a poem 'gifted' to them each day during the Advent period leading up to Christmas, December 1 to December 24. Forty some years later... my children still look forward each year to the poems that started a family tradition, that new generations have come to cherish.

It is my sincere hope that you will embrace and enjoy them, and share them with those you love.

Children of the Light was among the early poems I wrote, and is included in each of the *Poems of Life and Love* books in The Ellison Collection: *Heartstrings, Celebrations, Inspirations, Sanctuary, Awakenings, Sojourns, Milestones, Tapestry* and *Gratitude*. After writing many hundreds of poems, it is still my favorite. The words came from my heart... and my soul... and flowed so effortlessly that it was written in a single sitting. All I needed to do was capture the words on paper.

Light, to me, represented all that was good and pure and right with the world, and I believed then—as I do today—that those elements live in my children, and perhaps in all of us. We need only to dare.

– KCE

DEDICATION

To my parents: Herb and Bernice Haas

Mom, you were the poet who went before me...
unpublished, but appreciated nonetheless.

And Dad, you always believed in me,
no matter what direction my life took.
Thank you for your faith in me,
and for your unconditional love.

Table of Contents

Life's joys

Life's lessons

LIFE'S GIFTS

LIFE'S JOYS

GRATITUDE REVISITED

Gratitude unlocks the fullness of life;
It turns what we have into more.
It's the healthiest of all the human emotions,
The highest form of thought, and furthermore...
It's the greatest of virtues, the parent of all.
Gratitude helps us grow and expand;
It brings joy and laughter into our lives.
It makes sense of our past;
We know where we stand.

And as we express our gratitude
We must never forget this wisdom:
The highest appreciation for what we have
Is not to utter the words, but live by them.

A GOOD FRIENDSHIP

Good friends don't have to visit every day,
Or talk on the phone by the hour.
Some time might pass between conversations,
But when it picks up, it's at full power.

No person is your friend who demands your silence,
Or denies your right to grow.
A friend allows you to be perfectly yourself;
And shares in your good times and in your sorrow.

Having a good friend rates at the top of the chart;
It's one of the highest of life's delights.
To be a good friend can be a difficult undertaking,
But will take you to the noblest heights.

Friendship is built on two very important things:
Respect and trust, in like measure.
Friendship marks a life even more deeply than love.
The sharing of a friendship is a treasure.

CHILDREN OF THE LIGHT

There are those souls who bring the light,
Who spill it out for all to share.
And with a joy that does excite,
They show the world that they do care.
It is so very bright.

In this sharing, love does pervade
Into their lives and cycles round;
And as this light is outward played
The love is also inward bound.
It is an awesome trade.

You are a soul whose light is shared.
It comes from deep within your heart.
It's best because it is not spared,
Because it's total, not just part.
And I am glad you've dared.

TALENT

If you are born with a talent you are meant to use
Your greatest happiness will come from using it.
The artist is nothing without the talent,
And the talent is nothing unless you commit.

You are braver than you think and more talented than you know.
You're capable of more than you can imagine.
It's your motivation to succeed that carries you along,
And how well you do it your attitude will determine.

Some will say talent is an accident of genes,
And with that accident comes responsibility...
Responsibility to use it every way possible.
Don't hold back; share its wealth to the best of your ability.

Remember that you are talented, and your talent has value;
And that you are responsible for the talent you've been given.
What separates the talented one from a successful outcome
Is a lot of hard work; or so it is written.

GADGETS

When you dream, and you do, about the future coming up
There are gadgets everywhere, they do surround!
Each generation before us greeted change as well,
And the gizmos and the gadgets would only astound.

The radio, the telephone, and then Facebook! Oh my!
Each changed the world and sorta scared the old ones.
These gadgets were invented by people in their twenties!
And my take on this? They've only just begun!!!

There's another way of thinking about the onslaught of gadgets,
With their mesmerizing video displays:
Information is not knowledge and knowledge is not wisdom,
And wisdom is not foresight, by the way.

The gadgets provide us with leisure; they save us time;
But rarely do we have the silence in which to dream.
Radio and Sonos and big-screen televisions
Can keep us from our inner selves. (It would seem.)

So, balance is the answer in the management of our days,
We know there's something more than the best new thing.
The best gadget of all is the human brain,
With its creativity and its goal to make life sing.

CONTENTMENT

It's not what you have or what you are doing;
It's not who you are, or what you're pursuing
That brings happiness into your life every day!
It's what you think about it. Be grateful without delay!

Contentment doesn't mean you don't desire more!
It means you are thankful for what's come before!
You're also patient for what's coming your way,
And happy with what you have, every day.

An awareness of sufficiency, a sense of ˚enough˚
In both having and being (any more is just ˚stuff˚):
The simple gifts of life, like friendships and a good book,
A good laugh, a cold drink, or a murmuring brook.

Contentment allows you to experience satisfaction
Without obstructing dreams or thwarting interaction.
When you realize that there is nothing you need,
The whole world is yours. You may proceed.

KINDNESS

Kindness is the language which the deaf can hear;
And the blind can "see" kindness for more than a mile.
It is everything in life, the greatest of wisdoms.
The universal language of kindness is a smile.

Love and kindness are never wasted;
They bless both the "giver" and the "receiver."
Warm feelings occur, bringing a sense of peace.
Try it... and you'll become a believer.

There's no such thing as a small act of kindness.
A ripple is created with no logical end.
Like a pebble in a lake, the circle grows,
And touches another... a potential friend.

Constant kindness can accomplish much.
It can cause misunderstandings to evaporate.
A philosophy of kindness can be practiced anywhere.
Make it your simple religion to celebrate.

YOU MAY BE A MESSENGER

You understand that ordinary people
Are messengers of the Most High.
They unwittingly perform their miracles
Without seeming to bat an eye.
It's like a holy anonymity
As they go about their tasks.
It's not that they're trying to hide it.
They're not exactly wearing masks.

Yet if they had not been there at the time,
And had not said what they said,
Nor acted in such an amazing way,
It might have been something to dread.
And we would not be the way we are now
Without their presence at that moment.
And remember, they might not even be aware
Of the part they played when present.

Never forget you may be a messenger
Without being aware of it at all.
Think of an instance when someone said,
'You're an angel!' for picking up the ball.
Then look at your life and think of when
Someone's been an angel for you;
Whose been your messenger of the Most High
And helped to get you through.

THE TRUE JOY IN LIFE

Three things come to mind when thinking of what
I would include in my list of what brings joy.
I'm sure there are others, but I'll save them for later,
Not wanting to mislead you, or ever annoy.

The first one is being able to be used
For a purpose that I deem to be significant.
I'm limited only by my ability to imagine
This calling with my participation relevant.

Next, I want to be completely worn out
(Before I am thrown on the scrap heap),
With work for the good of people and the planet;
Then *scrapping* joyously. No need to weep.

And last, I want to be a force of nature,
Not a selfish little clod of complaints.
The world owes me nothing... not even happiness...
I earn it by working with egoless self-restraint.

UNBREAKABLE BONDS

Kind sentiment is nice, it sounds quite good,
But sentiment alone is not enough.
Without kind deeds to support the words
The likelihood of *true* friendship is rough.

If you're lucky enough to have a friend
Whose words and actions correspond,
Then you are blessed because you have
A special unbreakable bond.

And then if you are someone who returns in kind
This friendship of words *and* action,
Then you're someone who is in great demand.
You are a 'Center Ring' attraction.

RENEWAL

You can hardly wait for tomorrow because
It means a new life for you each day!
Renewal requires you to open yourself
To thinking and feeling in an entirely new way!

Life is the principle of self-renewal.
It is constantly renewing and transforming.
The greatest remedy in the world is change;
It's inevitable, and it enhances your performing.

Change brings you everything you could want,
And the source of all change is always internal.
It's the change from the within that first produces
The change in the without... a truth eternal.

Deep within the center of your being
Is the undaunted, the longing, the all-knowing...
The ready, the able, the perfect you
Waiting its turn to emerge—the next unfolding...
And the great unfurling of your wings to fly
And the reforged backbone of a true Child of Light.
Be willing to change and think the new of everything,
And you will walk through life with delight.

You will always be well, and will always have happiness;
You'll be free with an interesting life in balance.
You will constantly move forward into the larger;
And what you need today will be in abundance.

BE A FRIEND

As a friend you are someone who makes an effort
To be uplifting and kind.
You give other people a reason to trust,
As well as peace of mind.

Reach out to people who cannot smile
As you go on your walkabout;
And make it your practice to give to others
The benefit of the doubt.

Every new dawning holds a surprise;
Not much is "carved in concrete."
If you haven't made someone smile today,
Your day is not complete.

As you travel along your own path in life
Some friends go and some stay;
But if you hold friends very close to your heart
They'll never be far away.

THE POWER OF WORDS

Much attention is given to the moral Importance
Of our acts and deeds, and rightfully so, I am sure.
But in seeking the higher life we must consider
The moral power of the words that we utter!

One of the clearer marks of the moral life
Is right speech in our daily use.
'Think before speaking' is one of the ways
To make sure you're speaking with good purpose.

Glib talk disrespects others; breezy self-disclosure yourself.
The random dump of the content of one's mind
Is like a vehicle widely lurching out of control,
And destined for destruction of a kind.

Speech itself is neither good nor evil,
But it is used carelessly in every day interaction.
It is unbecoming to be a chatterbox.
Prattle defeats your higher purpose. It's a distraction.

PLAYTIME

Play energizes and enlivens. It eases your burden.
It opens you up to many a new possibility.
Play fosters belonging and encourages cooperation.
It's a requirement to bring out your creativity.

Carl Jung put it bluntly when he made the statement
That the intellect does not create something new.
No, ˙ ... it's accomplished by the play instinct.˙
It's been documented. No need to argue.

He went on to say that, ˙the debt we owe
To the play of the imagination
Is beyond measure; it's truly incalculable
For the advancement of civilization.˙

It's a happy talent to know how to play.
It's harder to maintain as you age.
Play keeps you fit, both physically and mentally.
Stay playful... you'll have a distinct advantage.

Play is training for the unexpected...
The things that send your schedule astray.
It's said the supreme accomplishment is
To blur the line between work and play.

If you want to be creative, stay in part a child.
The great man is he who does not lose his child's heart.
In our play we reveal what kind of people we are,
And what kind of legacy we will impart.

LIVE AND LET LIVE

If you live in the freedom
Of your own thoughts and desires,
You must allow that same freedom to others.
While you may wish that people
Have no judgments about you
You also must not judge your brothers.

Learn to accept
The behavior of others
That doesn't fit with what you believe.
See your opinion
As merely opinion,
Not truth, and not worthy of a peeve.

Others' opinions of you
And yours of others
Lead to useless, negative thought.
And the guilt and the fear
That results from this thinking
Lead not to the goals that are sought.

Life's lessons

CLEAR YOUR CALENDAR

It's easy to fill your calendar with events
Which require your attendance and dollars.
But be careful to keep ample time for yourself...
The obligations can feel like tight collars.

It's when you are quiet, and sometimes alone,
Or with loved ones close to your heart
That real communion takes place and the spirit is felt;
That the glow of inspiration can create art.

If you're over-scheduled and constantly running
Here and there, there and here, and back.
You'll miss the life-altering gifts which abound;
They'll come to you when you relax.

Make space in your life for no action at all!
Make leisure time part of your daily routine.
Let the Spirit in and listen to the message,
And enjoy those times serene.

INTERNAL DIALOGUE

Internal dialogue is what goes on
Inside your head between your ears.
It's what you're thinking about your life
And about the world, that no one hears.
You alone hear what you say.
No one else can read your thoughts.
It's your filter on how you see the world.
It's full of your "shoulds," your "oughts."
So it stands to reason, it would seem,
That control of your dialogue begins with you.
Remember, you're the one in charge
To change or keep that point of view.

PONDERING DEATH

Seldom do we stop to reflect,
When things are going well,
On loss or death or blindness.
On these we do not dwell.

But if you would, for just a bit,
Reflect with me as we glide
Along the following train of thought...
It could be an interesting ride.

What if death is not the greatest loss
In life, as we all thought to be true?
How about what dies inside us as we live
Being worse than death, for your clue?

And worse than death is being blind,
Immune to the joy of being alive.
Everything about life is miraculous,
From it all things good to derive.

So we must be diligent today
To keep from dying inside.
And look beyond our usual views
To that miracle. In you it resides!

QUESTIONS

Very few people really seek knowledge.
They approach the unknown with an agenda,
And try to wring answers they've already shaped
With justifications, confirmations, and addenda.

To really ask the question and being open to the answer
Might open the door to a whirlwind of wisdom.
The questions you ask of yourselves will determine
The type of people you will eventually become.

Remember this wisdom regarding your questions
(You'll have many of varying importance):
The most important ones in life can't be answered
By anyone except yourself. (Do the dance.)

It's the questions you can't answer that teach you the most.
They teach you how to think things through.
Given an answer, all you gain is a little fact.
But a question requires the most work from you.

Have patience with what remains unsolved in your heart.
Try to love the questions themselves.
Like locked rooms and books in another tongue,
Your search continues for yourselves.

LESSONS FROM NATURE

Just take a look around you
And study the Natural Way:
The light in the sky above you...
(From blue to dapple gray).
The unfolding of your ideas...
(Just short of miracle-play)!
The emptiness of space... (What is
Beyond the Milky Way)?
The fullness of all life...
(Though sometimes in disarray).
The behavior of Saints...
(Exemplary, I dare say)!

>   The events of Nature are potent!
>   There's hardly ever a quirk.
>   They always evolve in accordance
>   With how things work.

Imagine what would happen
If the processes were neurotic.
A lazy sky would flicker...
(The light would be spasmodic).
Your thoughts would be irrational...
(You'd feel quite idiotic).
Space could become agitated...
(And likely quite chaotic).
Life would seem quite useless...
(At best, only episodic).
The Saints you could not trust...
(They might become despotic).

> Potency comes from knowing
> And acting according to
> What is happening right now.
> The rest is up to you.

RESPONSIBILITY

There are really only two choices in life.
(The statement stands as a classic theorem):
To accept your life's conditions as they exist,
Or accept the responsibility to change them.

Responsibility is the thing people dread most of all,
But without taking it, self-respect won't develop.
By giving your responsibility to another entity,
It has the power over you, with no let-up.

Find joy in everything you choose to do...
Every job, relationship... or at home.
It's your responsibility to love it... or change it.
You alone can choose the outcome.

It's you who will get you where you want to go.
Nobody else has the power, or the right.
You are fully responsible for the choices you make;
Your positive direction will bring great delight.

Nothing strengthens the judgment or quickens the conscience
Like individual responsibility. One will adjust.
Few things can help an individual more than
To place responsibility on him, with trust.

Concern yourself more with accepting responsibility
Than assigning blame and calling it human nature.
The ability to accept responsibility in life
Is the measure of you alone. (For sure!)

IT'S JUST LIFE

Where on earth do we get the idea
That life should be fair, when it's not?
Is it possible we've been under the illusion
That fairness will be the outcome on the spot?

The thing that makes life seem unfair
Is that our thinking about fairness is defective.
Fairness is the way we think
Things should be... from our perspective.

What is important in life is life,
And not the results of living.
This is the only life we are sure of,
So live today; the gift is in the giving.

LOVE VS. CRITICISM

Whenever you see a need to "fix,"
Or to suggest to another a change,
Take a moment—and a breath—and ask yourself,
"Would this be a loving exchange?"

Sometimes our need to comment is stronger
Than our desire to keep the peace.
Words that wound instead of support
Could prompt mutual trust to cease.

Before you say anything, check your motives;
Make your words welcome and wise.
When dealing with loved ones, it's best to pause
And think before speaking. Otherwise,
Words that wound take a long time to heal
And more often than not can jeopardize
A trust that was established over time.
If you hurt their feelings, apologize!

MISFORTUNE

"Fire is the test of gold," it is said;
"Adversity, of strong men."
Seneca of distant pre-Christ days
Wrote those wise words with his pen.

Look at each misfortune you endure.
Study it carefully and seek to find
The fringe benefits—the lessons to learn.
Good from every setback can be mined.

There's a story of a miller, a grinder of grain,
Dependent upon the stream for his power.
A flood came along and washed away
His mill and all of his flour.

He lamented long hours, he cried up a storm,
Saying, "How could God do this to me?"
He felt helpless and hopeless as he stood on the site
Of what had once been his prosperity.

As his tears became dry and his eyes were clear
He looked around his former stronghold.
And glimmering there at the bank of the stream
Was a large deposit of gold.

That which impoverished him made him rich.
His plight (the flood) did reveal
What was there all the time, but covered up.
It took misfortune to make it real.

MARCEL PROUST ON BALANCE

"Le bonheur seul est salutaire pour le corps,
mais 'est le chagrin qui developpe les forces de l'esprit."*

Happiness and sorrow go hand in hand
In the development of the human supreme.
We need both in our lives to achieve balance
Between body and spirit, it seems.

Notice your body the very next time
You're ecstatic and jumping for joy;
You've no pains nor aches; you're made of steel,
And movement is the thing you enjoy.

But, "can you talk," or think deep thoughts
When your endorphins are racing around—
When every breath of new-found air
Helps to lift you off the ground?

Then notice your body when you feel pain,
When sorrow and grief fill your soul.
Your spirit is challenged to rise again.
Balance becomes your only goal.

Sorrow develops the powers of the spirit
And happiness benefits the body, pro tem;
It would be nice if we could have
Body and spirit together, in tandem.

*Translation: Happiness alone is good for the body,
but sorrow develops the spirit.*

NEGATIVE THINKING

Negative thinking can do more harm
And kill more people than combat.
It can promote conditions in human beings
Where infections and germs find habitat.

It's said that it comes from insecurity,
From feelings of not being good enough;
Low self-esteem and unworthiness,
Of not having "what it takes"—"the right stuff."

It's a vulture that sits there on your shoulder
Saying stupid things in your ear—
Like, "You're not good enough, you can't do the job."
It's a campaign designed to smear.

When one's upbringing is slanted more
Toward complaints and criticisms than praise,
The doubts set in and then, of course,
A lifetime can be filled with malaise.

You notice I said, "It can be filled
With malaise," not, "It will be so!"
You were given the power to change the way
To live your lives and to grow.

No matter the upbringing, you can choose to lose
The negative way of looking at things.
And if you do, you will find great joy—
Enough to notice your heart actually sings!

Risk taking

Life without risk is no life at all!
Yet, the further out on a limb, the more likely a fall.
But the fruit is sweeter the farther you climb.
You can't win without risking, most of the time.

'All life is an experiment!' So states Ralph Waldo...
And the more experiments, the better, was his motto.
Of course there is danger! But opportunity is also present!
The two are inseparable. The outcome can be magnificent!

You can't outwit fate by standing on the sideline,
And placing side bets, waiting for a sign
On the outcome of life, then expect to win big!
You must wade in and drink life! Take a big swig!

If you're not willing to risk the unusual
You'll settle for the ordinary, the ineffectual.
Like the line in the movie about two gals who wanted more...
Thelma and Louise said, "You get what you settle for."

Only those who risk going too far
Can find out how far one can go (toward a star?)
If you're offered a seat on a rocket ship, don't wait!
Don't ask which seat. Just get on! Don't be late!

GIVE YOUR UNIQUE GIFT

Each of us is blessed with a gift.
As we journey through life it becomes known.
Your gift is worth nothing 'til you give it away.
Watch the seeds grow as they are sown.

In the eyes of the world your gift may be small,
Or larger than any gift going.
But it matters not the size or scope.
What matters is your love outflowing.

It is through the finding and the giving
Of this gift with which you're blessed
That you find the joy that's at the core
Of being and doing your best.

Identify one talent that you possess
That has enriched the life of another.
Please rejoice in your ability to give.
It's unlike any other.

LIFE'S GIFTS

BELIEVE IN ABUNDANCE

What you enjoy, not what you have,
Is how your abundance is measured.
Your inner possessions, your gratitude for your blessings,
Are what bring the abundance to be treasured.

A generous heart filled with gratitude
Will always be the strongest magnet
For bringing abundance into your life.
Share lovingly and you'll have no regret.

Your ability to love and be loved in return—
An innate quality, not one that's acquired—
Will attract abundance, health, and happiness.
This is the law of Nature. Your life is inspired.

Doing what you love is the cornerstone for having
Abundance in your life on a daily basis.
When you are grateful your fears disappear,
And you are free to succeed (with emphasis).

Making a dream into a reality begins
With what you have when you start.
It's not dependent on what you're waiting for.
So get going—use your head and your heart!

THANK YOU, ERICH FROMM*

Man is the only animal for whom
His own existence is a problem...
A problem which must be solved by himself
Before he can build his life's totem.

If you are what you have, and you lose what you have,
Then who are you? A question to ponder...
Dig deep and find that you are what you are...
So, of yourself, grow fonder.

The task you must set for yourself is not
To strive to feel secure;
But to be able to tolerate insecurity
Whenever and wherever you adventure.

The quest for certainty blocks your search for meaning.
You can search through every resource.
But, uncertainty is the very condition that
Impels you to unfolding your "force."

Love is the union with something or someone
Outside yourself (as I am seeing);
But under the condition of retaining the separateness
And integrity of your own being.

The questions appear as you go through life.
You search high and low with persistence.
Love is the only sane and satisfying answer
To the problem of human existence.

Your main task in life is to give birth to yourself,
To become all you can potentially be.
The most important product of your effort
Is your own personality.

To die is poignantly bitter, you know.
Eventually we all must transcend;
But the idea of dying without having lived
Is unbearable to even comprehend.

*German Social Psychologist, Psychoanalyst, Sociologist
and Human Philosopher*

FRIENDS

The mysteries of life and death are many,
And sometimes too much to comprehend.
The journeys we make throughout our lives
Are more meaningful when shared with a friend.

Friends give substance to our joys and sorrows;
They make the road of life an easier trek.
We need each other to share this life—
Need each other to stay in check.

Friends bring joy and share our sorrows.
They are there for the sadness and the fun!
We need each other to share the journey
And to remind us that we are all one.

PEOPLE

Stress, anxiety, and depression are caused
When we are living just to please someone.
People in your life should be a valuable source
Of reducing stress, and providing you with fun.

It's okay to live a life others don't understand.
Standing alone is better than being undervalued.
If you're treated like an option, leave those people like a choice.
Moving on is your gift to you, as you are self-rescued.

You don't need to explain yourself to anyone.
You don't need their approval or their support.
Live your life and do the things that make you happy.
The results of your choices will bring you comfort.

REALITY

"There is no reality except in action."
To Sartre this quote is referenced.
Life is not a problem to be solved,
But a reality to be experienced.

Many philosophers have studied reality,
And consensus has seemed to rest
On the awareness that reality ebbs and flows...
A series of natural changes, at best.

Resisting the changes only creates sorrow,
And purloins your inherent vitality.
You are more often frightened than hurt, and you
Suffer more from imagination than reality.

Thinking something does not make it true,
And wanting something does not make it real.
The appearance of things changes according to emotions;
Your reality exists within, you will reveal.

Deep in your unconscious is a pervasive need
For a logical universe that makes sense.
Reality exits only a step beyond logic.
It's a persistent illusion, in essence.

YOURSELF

What's in you is the answer to your problems.
The solution has to come from within.
You hold all the answers regarding your path.
Listen to yourself and you will win.

Others outside can listen and advise,
But a solution they cannot give you.
You must see it through all the way by yourself,
And with courage you will come shining through.

It is more important to become and to be
Than to get and possess things galore.
What you carry inside will take you farther
Than what carries you to the door.

The mind is a powerful thing, as you know.
It can build barriers, and demolish them, too.
What happens to you in your life will be
A result of what's inside of you.

The story is about you, and you are the author.
It's a continuing script for your screenplay.
You direct it and edit it and present it to the world.
You're in charge of your life all the way.

The entire world is affected by what you are,
And what you are lies inside your mind.
You hold the key to unraveling it all,
As you make yours the truth that you find.

FEAR IS A FEELING

So just what is this thing called fear
That can have so strong a hold on us?
And, moreover, just where does it come from?
Did it arrive here on the 8:30 bus?

Our parents may have taught us to be afraid
Of temptations to danger that seemed inviting.
We were too young then to know the difference between
The legitimately dangerous and the merely exciting.

But as adults we can determine for ourselves
The difference between disaster and possibility.
Most fear is a myth of childhood comfort...
So is Santa, the Easter Bunny, and the Tooth Fairy.

Fear is a feeling, that's all it is.
It may make your stomach turn and churn.
But it cannot stop you in your endeavors.
Only you stop you in your sojourn.

IDENTIFY WITH YOUR STRENGTHS

Identify yourself with your full potential,
Not with a fault or mistake.
The first energizes and creates more good;
The other can leave you with heartache.

To identify yourself with weakness—
If even in the name of humility—
Is a negative image to adopt,
No matter the sake of civility.

Work with your strength, not your weakness,
Because if you don't, you'll appear
To accept weakness as your reality—
And happiness will elude you, I fear.

Believing

Believing is a daring adventure for us all.
It's a journey into the unseen.
It's a radiant faith in the yet undiscovered.
It's going where no one has been.

There's magic, my loves, in the art of uncertainty.
"All things are possible to those who believe."
The Master Himself said those words long ago.
Through our consciousness the meaning does weave.

Believe in the limitless supply of God's goodness.
His wonders abound everywhere.
Believe in yourself and your goals in life.
Believe to achieve, and you'll dare.

Believe that you have whatever it takes
And it will be there at your command.
Have faith in others and they'll have faith in you.
Giving and receiving go hand in hand.

"You may be deceived if you trust too much,"
Was the advice of one Frank Crane,
"But you'll live in torment if you don't trust enough."
You'll lose much less than you gain.

Believe in life's enduring values...
In the good of all mankind.
Stand up and be counted for the things that count.
The peace will still your mind.

Believe that you are quite enough
In order to succeed.
Believe that supply will be at hand
For anything you'll need.

Believe, my loves. The magic of believing
Is for you and you alone.
You're the captain of your ship... you stand at the helm.
For your own lives you set the tone.

FRIENDSHIP EXCHANGE

A life without friends is hard to imagine,
But it sounds like a horrible thing.
It would be like a house with no foundation
That in a storm would go vanishing.

Strong relationships are like a strong fortress;
They keep out influences you don't want.
And the more friends you have, the better you'll be
Fortified against things unpleasant.

Draw from others where you are weak;
And give to them where you are strong.
This exchange of care and nurturing
Paves the way for a friendship long.

A CLOSING THOUGHT

POETRY

It's the revelation
Of a sensation
That the poet
(Wouldn't you know it)
Believes to be
Felt only interiorly
And personal to
The writer who
... writes it.

It's the interpretation
Of a sensation
That was fueled by
A poet's sigh
And believed to be
Shared mutually
And personal to
The lucky one who
... reads it.

About the author

Kathryn Carole Ellison is a former newspaper columnist
and journalist and, of course, a poet.

She lives near her children and stepchildren and their families in the
Pacific Northwest, and spends winters in the sunshine of Arizona.

You might find her on the golf course with friends, river rafting, traveling
the world, writing poems... or enjoying the Opera and the Symphony.

Late bloomer

Our culture honors youth with all
It's unbridled effervescence.
We older ones sit back and nod
As if in acquiescence.

And when our confidence really gels
In early convalescence...
"We can't be getting old!" we cry,
"We're still struggling with adolescence!"

Acknowledgments

I have many people to thank...

First of all, my amazing children—Jon and Nicole LaFollette—for inspiring the writing of these poems in the first place. And for encouraging me to continue my writing, even though their wisdom and compassion surpass mine... and to my dear daughter-in-law and friend, Eva LaFollette, whose encouragement and interest are so appreciated.

My wonderful stepchildren, Debbie and John Bacon, Jeff and Sandy Ellison, and Tom and Sue Ellison who, with their children and grandchildren, continue to be a major part of my life; and are loved deeply by me. These poems are for you, too.

My good friends who have received a poem or two of mine in their Christmas cards these many years, for complimenting me on the messages in my poems. Your encouragement kept me writing and gave me the courage to publish.

To Kim Kiyosaki who introduced me to the right person to get the publishing process under way... Mona Gambetta with Brisance Books Group. I marvel at her experience and know-how to make these books happen.

To Amy Anderson, Sonya Kopetz, Kerri Kazarba Schneider, and Ingrid Pape-Sheldon, my very creative public relations team of experts, who have carried my story to the world.

And finally, to John B. Laughlin, a fellow traveler in life, who encourages me every day in the writing and publishing process. John, I love having you in my cheering section.

BOOKS OF LOVE
by Kathryn Carole Ellison

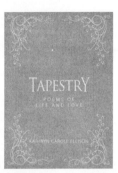

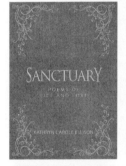